T0353156

the flap pamphlet series

Every Single One

flap

open, read, turn

Every Single One

the flap pamphlet series (No. 3)
Printed and Bound in the United Kingdom

Published by the flap series, 2011
the pamphlet series of flipped eye publishing
All Rights Reserved

Cover Design by Petraski
Series Design © flipped eye publishing, 2010

First Edition
Copyright © Nina Bahadur 2011

ISBN-13: 978-1-905233-35-9

LOTTERY FUNDED

Every Single One

Nina Bahadur

Contents | *Every Single One*

I Have Learned

I tell you I have learned what it's like
to be careful: it's not living.

You roll over. You are mindlessly
counting my ribs. You ask *what is, then?*

Running my tongue over clean teeth. A wet
leaf stuck to the bottom of my boot. Chilblains,

red fingertips in your mouth. A head rush,
magic words. Knowing exactly what you mean.

That heavy feeling in my stomach when I swallow
a whole Blue Moon in one minute. Clothes

right out of the dryer. Nutmeg on my coffee.
Spelling out words with stones in the woods.

Air so cold it shocks you. Candles in white paper
bags, all the way down Main Street, in the dark.

Every Single One

Today I am eighteen with a stamped
hand and bitten lips and my phone jammed
into the side of my dress. We're all dancing,
crushed and close. The boys I know are here
and I'm in hazy love with every single one;
they're generous with cocktails and
kisses on cheeks, happy-birthday-darlings,
an arm around my shoulders – *cheers*.

West London tonight is blurred and I am
laughing, dissipating into the flush. Out
on the street a boy holds my hand and I'm looking at
brittle grey trees, framed in stone squares.
I like to think about their bursting roots
coiling around each other under the pavement,
rising up, making the concrete buckle until
the road tilts into Wonderland

for me to slide into. I blink and then
someone is tugging on my elbow and
thumbing through my heart to stretch it out and
stop, one second, I'm out of
breath with sparks behind my eyes. When
I move my bones click like they were unlinked
and strung back together while I slept, and I
am waking now.

Paper Nest

I want what I want. And that's
to be young and have a heart,
to be smart and tell the truth,

with no one grabbing at me.
Once I felt thin and torn up in a
pale paper nest I built myself

and I was a bunch of apples, I
was Christmas-tree baubles,
shaken too hard – overpicked –

24b Winchester Square

The upstairs bathroom is loud this
New Years' Eve. The tub is filled with
ice and wine, and the feet

of girls sitting on the windowsill
are perched on the porcelain lip
like wooden elephants lined up

on the mantelpiece downstairs. Music
pulses through from the corridor and
wraps around a boy's legs as he walks

up to me. I speak over my shoulder; I
knew him as a child; my blood is electric
at remembering. People

dance in the doorframe, and
through the open window slides
the winter wind. It strikes a match.

Heat

It starts off straight.
You are well-mannered, a fish of a boy,
cool in redbricked streets baked between lines
marking us in and out.
In a choked café with tiled walls and curtains closed you tell me
I like the shapes of your legs in the dirt
and running circles round you
and your godhonest heartbeat and that's enough for me.
In black and breathless nights
I take your wrist, and I kiss, and the stars
are just pedestrians and the frantic sun
a bystander in the grand scheme of things that is us.
We blaze on through the dust
and burn in every bright afternoon.

When the storm breaks the land learns to drink
and for blurred August weeks we're sewn in by the rain.
When it's all hung out to dry
words drip from my lips, unsaid, I'm drowning,
and glass sunken in old windows makes the world
seem stranger.

All autumn steam rises:
washed out by the downpour, I let you go.
But there's a pale reminder cross-legged on your lawn,
your flickering morning memory, like light on scales,
of gasping for air, of skin on sheets.

Sunburn

Let's talk about us. The summer we spent
watching clouds, floating still in the water

together. Your fingers bunched
and brushed over mine before a few

tight midnights drinking in stale hotels
that we were just a bit young for

and your bottom lip between my teeth.
Just once. I still think about it. The endless

grey limbo, the numbered rooms, the
cold voices on the line. Getting lost.

You said the world would burn me up.
Now, sometimes, before I sleep, I find I'm

thinking about the future, waiting for
yellow walls and starfish hands grabbing,

and how the sun and the city, sticky,
will peel off leaving reddened skin

that I will press cold towels to
before turning off the light.

A Wise Woman Always Told Me

to say my prayers before I went to sleep
(long after I stopped believing that
anyone was listening). She said:
nightmares come from the heart.
Make sure you don't have secrets.

Too bad she never explained how
you share a twin extra-long
with someone six-foot-one.
Would mother really know best
how to stack two bodies
in such a space?

Would she understand that
sometimes we are close enough
for me to feel your bad dreams
crawling over me and seeping into my pores
like bad river air in the morning?
I wake feeling moldy and sleep again,
to dream about sleeping more;
suspended in warm darkness
hearing your heartbeat and your blood.
Let's just lie here, breathe in and out,
and grow.

Morse Code

You wrote this for me, said it aloud against my mouth
one night, measured my ear with your thumb and pointing
finger, bit your lip and opened your mouth.

You didn't know why or how but
when you closed your eyes with me
your heart beat out my name in morse code,

in binary, in Chinese telegraph characters and
electric shocks, and you wanted to sing,
off-key, in the dark, about it.

Waiting

is terrible. I pick lint from my dress,
I file my nails. My horoscope tells me
"You feel like you are peeling.
You are still there underneath."

For fifty-five minutes at 350°,
I bake *coming-home pie*. I play it
by ear with pecans, a nectarine, and
the hold music at American Airlines.

The tongues of bells lick me
awake each morning. I look
for signs in vapor trails that
cross and fade.

I scrub the house with Brillo pads,
I keep the windows open.
I don't want you to smell
the musk of rotten fruit;
to understand how I am limited
by loving.

Baby, Will You Help Me

zip this dress; will you not
get drunk tonight and will you
please just hold my hand?
Tomorrow I'm flying home, so

instead of going out with you I'll
be hiding meat in my napkin at
a welcome-back party. I'm
excited, I promise, so happy
to be here. But it seems I'm

not grown-up yet, it seems
that I drink keg beer
and use vulgar American
words. I'm too fresh,
and the way I say just what
I mean is all of a sudden
offensive in my
rhotic pronunciation, my
up-and-down intonation.

And, you're right, I've known them
all for years. I grew up in their
houses, I played in their gardens,
I could take it or leave it.
I wouldn't mind if they stared, but –

I'll be far from you. Your voice
will sound wrong on the phone, and
I won't see that first morning look –

today, your eyes opened like you'd been
falling face-first.

Overflow

We come in from the floods, faces flushed, shoes
trailing wet laces over the carpet. Jammed cheek
to cheek in the front hall my fingers fumble with
buttons. You curse, soft. I hang dripping clothes
on stairs and banisters, going up backwards, skin
tingling in the air. Leaning over the bath there are
goosebumps and my toes sucked to the tiles. Your
shape in the doorway is sorry.

Next morning all the ceilings are damp, steamed
wallpaper curling at corners. At the bleached
sink I'm rinsing my heart out, wringing, feeling
under my fingers the patterned throbs – a fish
flopping out of water, the beat of spring rain.

Take the Hand You are Dealt

1.
"Laws of magnetism? I couldn't explain them
with my hands. Here's what I know: I'm drawn
to you."

2.
The cinema. Her tongue is cringing, dry,
from popcorn salt and recycled air, and
she's breathless from the gentle pressure
of five foreign fingers on her knee.

3.
Here are the rules: a bird in the hand
is worth two in the bush. And this is
what is hardest: to close the open
hand because one loves.

4.
How often do you think about that
night? The car door left a scar on
my ring finger.

5.
Love is one of those things; you don't have a choice.
I remember the first time that I heard your voice.
I've dreamt all night of golden wedding bands.
Enough with Petrarch. I love you for your hands.

6.
Dear J,
I'm sorry if this is illegible. I'm not
used to writing with my left hand yet.

7.
We fall asleep side-by-side and wake up
tangled, redfaced, cramped. Your grip
on my waist is vise-like – a man about to
fall, fingers grasping the edge.

Faces

The room is wrecked, a sign of what's to come,
littered with slack tights and wilted dresses ready
to sheathe me and turn me into someone

else. We drink yellow wine from the bottle
on the dresser, make silent toasts. Here's
to being young. The music in the background
is electric, urging us to go out and writhe

all over boys, take off our clothes, and *love* it.
Six girls, twelve limp black legs. The bathroom
mirror, the mirror above the bar, the mirror
in the club, all fogged and faces lost.

And now I want to be fresh again, not here, not this,
peeling a dress from sallow arms, awkward
elbows and fingers dry from clutched cigarettes.
My mouth tastes of night, of gum, of tongue,
I am sickly from hours of talk and stale air.

I want to take myself home, feet
throbbing with every step until I reach
the shower which always rings, alarmed,
and heaves water over my shoulders until
steam suffocates me then spits me out.

I am always the same at that time of un-morning
away from the streetlights all over the city.
Just me in my skin again, scrubbed, stainless
and new there: quiet. Close your eyes.

Sweetly

Do you remember? We spoke together,
sweetly. Words fell out about the people
I'd kissed, the pillows I smelled, the places
I was sick. And you smoked out the details.

My pomegranate shampoo, red rain-boots
in the back of the car, your hands
signing every word in the rented room.

Now, your space is hollow – my mouth
is shut. The longer I hold my breath,
the more I disappear. And I

count bites, I count drinks, I count beats, my
legs give way on the stairs.

The Squeeze

I'm getting it together. I start
with breathing, a choke-and-push,

letting things twist into focus.
Harsh light-circles, your face

floating close and being
pulled far away again.

Thinking is too hard. Your shoulder
is driftwood, bleached and

out of my grasp. If you won't
help, then I won't breathe.

I could swim out of this, but I'd
rather stay down here in the dark

waiting for something to rip
me away, to grab my blue heart

and start squeezing. Right now
I'm shaking and shivery. I need:

one, someone to tell me what to do,
and two, you.

Spin

The sun slides down your spine and sticks at your heels.
In dreams, I find you twisting all the roads, cutting maps,
smashing down every bulwark I've built. Serpent in hand.
Oh boy. You ask me what this is, and I spin, and I say:

> it's a gold rush a protest march a marathon a fire alarm
> a falling city a meteorite a trip to the god damn moon.

I'm sick of your piousness, this off-kilter gospel,
you put me up too high. I'm carping from my citadel.

> My skin is flushed your ring is cold my heart accelerates
> and what are you looking at anyway?

You try to drain me down the sink, keep me in a drawer,
kiss me on her roof, and *oh* that charlatan's grin,
those puppeteer's hands. Those nights when the numbers
blur on your neon clock I say we are done.
But you sit up with dares and dreams and that
all-enticing wrong and you name all my bones and Lord
only knows how.

Yellow Weeks

Today I stepped over a paving stone that read
HOPE IS NOT ENOUGH. But it is,

during all these yellow weeks I've been waiting.
I saw you last through the plexiglass window
of the Circle Line train going Eastbound.
You smiled. You call me from a payphone

every two days to tell me about the eerie quiet,
the thirsty girls you meet and the limp feeling
you get after kissing them, like they have drunk
you dry.

I've been biting my nails, a raw galaxy, my hands.
There is writing on a blue house in Notting Hill.
It says I LOVED YOU;
of course I did.

I Tried To Give Up Writing

I am busy, very busy, sleeping and studying
and drinking and dressing up and down to
go up- and downtown. My head is full of
grade boundaries, shots, three-month rules.

I have no time for notebooks, for cafés, for
scribbles on the 9,10 or 27. Poems are replaced
by lists. Time alone, once spent thinking, is now
time spent with him, time spent not thinking.
I have plans to make, a world to move across.

I have a dream where it's dark and I am
alone and unsteady. I am tilting and
rocked back, violent

as if the century has taken me by the
shoulders and is shaking, *Can you hear
me? Are you listening?*

I am shook. I can hear you. I am listening.